T0347580

THE
RANGE ROVER
STORY

THE
RANGE ROVER
STORY

GILES CHAPMAN

The History Press

First published 2019

The History Press
The Mill, Brimscombe Port
Stroud, Gloucestershire, GL5 2QG
www.thehistorypress.co.uk

© Giles Chapman, 2019

The right of Giles Chapman to be identified as the Author
of this work has been asserted in accordance with the
Copyright, Designs and Patents Act 1988.

All rights reserved. No part of this book may be reprinted
or reproduced or utilised in any form or by any electronic,
mechanical or other means, now known or hereafter invented,
including photocopying and recording, or in any information
storage or retrieval system, without the permission in writing
from the Publishers.

British Library Cataloguing in Publication Data.
A catalogue record for this book is available from the British Library.

ISBN 978 0 7509 8923 7

Typesetting and origination by The History Press
Printed in China

CONTENTS

Introduction   6

1 Land Rover Pioneers: Four-Wheel Drive in Peacetime   8
2 Bridging the Gap Between Car and Off-Roader   17
3 British Flair and Ingenuity Forge a World-Beating Design   27
4 The Range Rover: A Blazing Success in the 1970s Gloom   38
5 Luxury and Prestige to the Fore in the 1980s and '90s   56
6 P38A and the Tricky Business of Updating an Icon   74
7 Back on Top, Minus Chassis, as the Marque Expands   84
8 The Radical, Compact Evoque Proves a Smash Hit   98
9 All-Aluminium Masterpiece and the Shock of the Velar   112

Today, Range Rover is an entire range of four-wheel drive vehicles serving everyone from the suburban family to rock 'n' roll royalty, via the landed gentry. While their design is beautifully executed and their finish gleaming, they all possess exceptional off-road capability. Modern Range Rovers face plenty of rivals, but it's all too easy to forget that the original version, launched in 1970, actually created the luxury sport-utility vehicle market from scratch. It was a brilliant piece of design (conceived in Britain on the customary shoestring) because its form so closely followed its function. It was ultra-capable but also highly sophisticated. No wonder the originals have soared in value recently as collectors realise the Range Rover truly is an automotive icon. As the marque phenomenon powers into its sixth decade, this book is a timely and concise reminder of all that it's achieved since a tight-knit group of Rover engineers first turned their thoughts to something very different ...

Range Rover generations.

You could pick from two convincing start points to the Range Rover's story, both many years before this groundbreaking British car was even imagined.

The first, 1930, appears positively antediluvian for a vehicle launched four whole decades later, but it's very relevant. It was when the Rover Company's manager Spencer Wilks and his brother Maurice Wilks, chief engineer, were elevated from being key personnel to actually guiding the carmaker's fortunes, as they became Rover board members.

Henceforth, they decided Rover would avoid any follies in the mass-production market by concentrating on high-quality cars based on excellent engineering. They would forgo left-field distractions and target wealthier customers; this solid strategy, and profits, put Rover on a sound footing for years to come. Britain's middle-class professionals – doctors, solicitors, accountants, civil servants, minor gentry even – became loyal marque devotees, and Rover built itself a superb reputation.

The second, 1948, was Rover's launch of the Land Rover.

The Second World War radically altered the company's outlook. Its engineering thoroughness had been diverted into jet-engine development and then production of Meteor tank power units. It acquired two brand-new plants in Birmingham, 'shadow factories' funded by the British government in the build-up to taking on Germany with home-grown military expertise.

When peace returned to Europe, the firm possessed some superb facilities but faced a dilemma. It had to provide evidence of a realistic export plan for its traditional saloon cars to central government, or else allocations of materials in short supply, such as steel, would be withheld. Although Rover could return easily to making 15,000 cars annually, the sober 10, 12, 14 and 16 models had limited potential in world markets, and the company's cautious forecasts meant it was permitted only enough steel to make just 1,100 a year. Rover needed something extra to keep its new Solihull factory

humming, and fortunately Maurice Wilks had a brainwave one day while working the land on his remote farm on Anglesey.

▲ The very first Land Rover prototype was envisaged as a hybrid pick-up/tractor, hence the central driving position.

▼ Four-wheel drive versatility was provided for farmers for the first time in the original Land Rover, here in Series I form.

On his 250 acres, Wilks used an army-surplus Willys Jeep as a runabout. He naturally found the four-wheel drive in this light ex-military vehicle perfect for his muddy fields, and it was massively more manoeuvrable and versatile than a tractor. Yet it was far from reliable and often in for repair at Rover's service department, where spare parts had to be handmade to keep it running. Wilks couldn't buy an alternative because there simply wasn't one. And that gave him the idea that here was Rover's opportunity. Legend has it the Wilks brothers drew their first concept sketches in the sand of a Welsh beach for a hybrid pick-up/tractor, and quickly decided this venture was a feasible stopgap product until steel restrictions eased.

The company's board gave its agreement in September 1947 for 'an all-purpose vehicle on the lines of the Willys-Overland post-war Jeep'. This statement meant exactly what it said, because for the first prototype, running a few months earlier, a Jeep chassis with its 80in wheelbase was actually used, complete with its original front and back axles. The engine, though, came from the Rover 10 car, and the single seat with a central driving position like a tractor pointed directly towards the potential market: farmers and landowners.

The prototype soon evolved away from being merely a Rover-powered Jeep. The engine was superseded

During the freezing night of 6/7 December 1995 three men were shot as they sat in a Range Rover on a farm track in Rettendon, Essex. Tony Tucker, Pat Tate and Craig Rolfe were all drug dealers. In January 1998 Michael Steele and Jack Whomes got life for the murders, based on evidence given by getaway driver-turned-supergrass Darren Nicholls, but their families insisted they were innocent. This complex tale inspired a film, *Essex Boys*.

by the 1.6-litre motor from the new Rover 60, which gave more torque, along with its four-speed gearbox and back axle. For power to the front axle, an overrun freewheel was incorporated into a special low/high-range transfer case to give permanent four-wheel drive without a centre differential. The front axle disengaged from the manual transmission on the overrun, so the front wheels could revolve faster than the rear ones, Meanwhile, a simple ring-pull mechanism locked the freewheel for four-wheel drive. This meant downhill engine braking worked only through the rear wheels.

The centre-steer layout was quickly abandoned because the vehicle was easier to engineer with a normal, offset steering column. However, countrymen didn't want for versatility, as power take-off points were incorporated front, centre and rear, which could motorise agricultural machinery like welding equipment or a circular saw.

Armed with defence-industry knowledge, Rover knew there was plenty of war-surplus aluminium readily available and so, apart from the galvanised-steel box-section chassis, it fashioned the simple bodywork from sheets of aircraft-grade 'Birmabright' aluminium-magnesium alloy; these could be made by staff using simple hand tools without commitment to costly stamping equipment. Indeed, the only major component needing

➤ The very first thoughts about a more civilised Land Rover came in 1948 with the expensively coach-built Station Wagon.

You've never owned a car so useful, so practical

NO sedan can match a station wagon for all-round usefulness. And no other station wagon is so practical for every use as the "Jeep" Station Wagon—the first with an all-steel body and top for greater safety and longer service. It's a roomy, comfortable family car. When you need extra big load space, all except the driver's seat are removable. Let your Willys-Overland dealer show you how fully the "Jeep" Station Wagon meets your family's needs.

LOTS OF ROOM inside the "Jeep" Station Wagon's all-steel body for passengers—space, too, for things you want to take along. When there's a bulky load to haul, such as a chair or washing machine to be repaired, removing the seats gives 96 cubic feet of cargo space.

WONDERFULLY SMOOTH RIDING on country roads as well as city streets. Independent front-wheel suspension absorbs road bumps, keeping the car level and steady. It's a thrifty car to drive—the world-famous "Jeep" Engine with overdrive delivers mileage to brag about.

LET IT SNOW or rain or the sun beat down—the "Jeep" Station Wagon's all-steel body and top can take it. Even more important, you drive a "Jeep" Station Wagon with the secure feeling of sturdy steel around and above you.

'Jeep' Station Wagon

WITH STEEL BODY AND TOP

WILLYS-OVERLAND MOTORS, TOLEDO
MAKERS OF AMERICA'S MOST USEFUL VEHICLES

tooling was the transmission transfer case – everything else was either off-the-shelf or easily and cheaply fabricated.

In the end, although the 80in wheelbase was retained, no Willys Jeep parts were used. The whole production-ready vehicle, now called the Land Rover, was created in seven months, and the wraps came off it at the Amsterdam Motor Show on 30 April 1948. It was just eighteen months since Maurice Wilks first conceived it.

In July 1948, the definitive Land Rover was launched, appropriately, at the Bath & West Agricultural Show. The £540 price tag was free of Purchase Tax (an ancestor of VAT) because it was purely a commercial vehicle, and not a car. The two-seater pick-up came with a rudimentary canvas hood and was available only in dark green (army-surplus materials again – ex-Avro Aircraft paint).

Driving the Land Rover off-road was truly a revelation. Although heavier than the Willys Jeep, the 50bhp engine with its meaty 80lb ft of torque at 2,000rpm meant the Land Rover could easily bound up slippery hills on its Avon Trackgrip tyres. The industrial-strength leaf-spring suspension front and back nonetheless allowed excellent wheel articulation, while the approach/departure angles of 45/35 degrees meant the Land Rover could hop nimbly over ruts and small boulders. The only downside was hill-descent, as the front and rear wheel speeds were somewhat uncoordinated. However, once mastered, drivers could handle that. And it could return a decent 24mpg.

The Range Rover had a starring role in *Octopussy* in 1983. Roger Moore as James Bond kicked off a spectacular stunt sequence in an Acrostar mini-jet plane, escaping a heat-seeking missile launched from a trailer tugged by a specially built Range Rover convertible.

◄◄ In the USA, Jeep's steel-panelled Station Wagon of 1946 was sold on practicality and low prices.

Farmers had never known anything like it and immediately saw how the dual-purpose Land Rover could transform rural life. It was perfectly suitable for road use when a regular or occasional trip into the nearest market town was required, perhaps towing a cattle trailer or horsebox.

Production began with the aim of selling fifty Land Rovers a week. But then a funny thing happened. After a few weeks, output had to double to match the orders, and shortly they doubled again. By the end of the financial year 1948–49, Rover had sold 8,000 Land Rovers against an already raised projection of 5,000; by 1950–51, output had doubled once more to 16,000 and Land Rovers were out-selling Rover cars by two to one.

The company had a serious hit on its hands. Land Rovers started to be acquired by building contractors, police forces, electricity boards and, by the 1950s, the British Army. Anyone who needed light transport over tricky terrain simply had to have one.

The Land Rover was built for hard graft. Driver and passenger comfort were a low priority, along with style, as the four-wheel drive took it to places other vehicles couldn't reach. But things were about to change, just a little.

The general perception of Land Rovers, even among knowledgeable enthusiasts, is that the vehicles evolved slowly and stuck closely to the original, working-tool ethos. And yet, even in the first year of manufacture, Rover was gauging the market for something to bridge the chasm between utility and luxury. In October 1948, at the London Motor Show, the company revealed a bold new idea in the form of its seven-seater Land Rover 80in Station Wagon. The bodywork nose profile was as before but the pick-up bed had been transformed with four extra passenger seats, while the attractive bodywork, from coachbuilder Tickford, was panelled in aluminium on an ash wood frame, just as on a contemporary, hand-crafted limousine. Inside, luxury touches included high-quality leather upholstery, a heater, and a one-piece laminated windscreen. The side-facing rear seats could fold to create cargo space. On the outside, the usual spare wheel carried on the bonnet was encased in a stylish metal cover.

This model wasn't cheap. The £959 price (including £209 purchase tax) reflected the craft that went into building it. Only 641 were sold over three years, with a mere fifty going to British buyers. It was regarded as expensive at home. In the USA, Jeep launched its own station wagon at a much more affordable price (although never sold in Britain) because its body used was made of metal pressings rather than coach-built panels. After a hiatus of three years, Land Rover revisited the Station Wagon idea, after introducing mechanical improvements that included replacing the freewheel with a dog-leg clutch to give selectable four-wheel drive and four-wheel engine braking, a more powerful 2-litre engine and a beefier chassis with increased wheelbases.

New for '54, the 86in short-wheelbase Station Wagon had three doors and was joined a year later by the 107in five-door model. Unlike the elegant Tickford, these had aluminium bodies of extreme boxiness, with severe right-angles, sheer profiles and exposed rivets showing that they were built in-house on the same simple basis as other Land Rovers. Interiors and fittings were far from sumptuous, while the longer of the two was essentially a crew bus, seating ten people in cramped discomfort. Both could be ordered with a raised 'Safari' roof – an additional outer layer of tough leathercloth-type material keeping the interior cool in baking heat and reducing condensation in winter, plus an interior roof vent that let in air and not rain.

With starting prices down to £893 for the 86in Station Wagon, Land Rover's passenger-focused models now found a wide and receptive market. For many people living out in the sticks, they now

➤➤ In 1954, Land Rover revisited the Station Wagon concept by building them cheaply in-house; this is the 88in short-wheelbase model.

made an excellent alternative to a conventional large estate car, although most Station Wagons were used as pure working vehicles, especially by important fleet buyers such as the RAF.

Maurice and Spencer Wilks, and their Land Rover, had turned the Rover Company into a shining success story in Britain's often-troubled motor industry. Yet they'd envisaged the Land Rover as a short-lived sideline and were in perpetual fear of its appeal falling away – even though it never did. Like all clever operators they formed contingency plans.

For Pope John Paul II's visit to Britain in 1982, the government commissioned two special 'Popemobiles' from Ogle Design, with a platform from which the pontiff could wave to the crowds, bulletproof glass to 'heart level', a rear platform for riding security guards, run-flat tyres and a police radio. The Vatican was so impressed it bought it afterwards.

One of them was to lead the field in the untapped potential of gas turbine 'jet' engines for road vehicles, and in 1950 they amazed the world by unveiling the world's first jet-powered car, called Jet 1. In 1952, this open two-seater caused global excitement when it set a new land-speed record for gas turbines at 152mph; you can still pay homage to this British pioneer at the Science Museum in London, where it's on permanent display.

Another idea was to create a sort of halfway house between a Land Rover and a Rover car. Initial thoughts were for a compact vehicle using some of the simple manufacturing techniques and tall, roomy proportions of the Land Rover, but relying on conventional Rover car drivetrain and chassis, with rear-wheel drive only. A prototype was built and nicknamed the 'Greenhouse' for its shed-like proportions and sliding windows. The project was largely the work of Rover engineer Gordon Bashford but, once it was clear Land Rover demand showed absolutely no sign of sagging, the impetus for the vehicle weakened. The Wilks' worries were proving groundless.

And yet …

Despite the relative failure of the Tickford, the success of the austere Station Wagons, and tepid enthusiasm for the 'Greenhouse', Rover strategists instinctively felt there was still a market awaiting exploitation for a kind of crossbreed – something

fusing the best of Rover cars' comfort and elegance with the high-riding usefulness of a Land Rover.

By 1955, under Bashford's care again, the car was back in the frame and starting to be called the Road-Rover. The all-new P5 3-Litre saloon was heading towards its launch in three years' time, and a completely rethought Road-Rover now took shape as its stablemate. This was a handsome dual-purpose, two-door vehicle on a 98in wheelbase, and a tailgate split between drop-down metal lower and a flip-up glazed upper sections. Running prototypes were built, with drive to the rear wheels only, and Bashford drove one on a daily basis. Among its high-technology features were front disc brakes. Rover was so confident the car would succeed that work got underway to put it on sale by 1960 ... only for the unlucky Road-Rover to be shunted into the sidings again as the even more radical P6 saloon took precedence. You can see how tantalisingly close the Road-Rover came to showroom reality when you look at the surviving prototype today in the British Motor Museum in Gaydon, Warwickshire.

The P6, as the Rover 2000, went on to be a huge hit after launch in 1963. It set the template for the sporty executive four-door saloon later copied by everyone from Ford to BMW, and established Rover as a company bursting with cutting-edge thinking, and an uncanny way to put it in drivers' hands.

◄◄ A 107in long-wheelbase Station Wagon, fully showing its utilitarian nature and workmanlike construction method.

On 3 December 1971, a British Army team set off with two Range Rovers to drive the 14,000-mile length of the Americas, from Anchorage to Cape Horn. The most challenging part was the crossing of the Darién Gap, a 250-mile stretch of swamp and jungle south-east of the Panama Canal, with no roads. They carried inflatable boats for crossing deep water and aluminium ladders to use as portable bridges, reaching Cape Horn on 10 June 1972.

Meanwhile, though, the Americans had stolen a march on a Road-Rover-type vehicle. The International Harvester Scout of 1961 was the first true so-called 'sport-utility vehicle', but it was the 1963 Jeep Wagoneer and 1964 Ford Bronco that started to appear on suburban driveways across the USA. Derived from pick-up trucks, these lofty four-wheel-drive estate cars swiftly grew in appeal. Doubtless, many were bought because their owners lived in inhospitable outposts where four–driven wheels and huge rock-hopping ground clearance were essential. But many more were now proudly owned by families who liked visiting the great American outdoors of unmade tracks, plus the

▲ The 'Greenhouse' Road-Rover running prototype, considered a halfway-house between a Land Rover and a Rover car. Photo courtesy Graham Robson.

▲ The second-generation Road-Rover prototype was much more ambitious, and almost made it into production in 1960. Photo courtesy Graham Robson.

occasional trek through woodland or across mud, sand or shingle. The Wagoneer and Bronco were excellent for towing caravans, boats and kayak trailers, and reassuring to drive when it was snowing or stormy. A Land Rover could equal or beat them in sheer off-road capability, but its on-road performance was secondary, downright uncomfortable over long journeys, and passenger comfort and accommodation was comparatively terrible.

Rover, it concluded, could now really do with something to crack the American market for itself, since its sophisticated saloon cars had limited appeal there against Detroit's established heavy metal, which included sudden and 'disruptive' smash hits such as the Plymouth Barracuda and Ford Mustang. Rover's market research found demand for off-road cars like the Wagoneer was growing constantly. And those Road-Rover plans were still in the metaphorical bottom drawer …

The Range Rover Velar SVR, with supercharged 5-litre V8 engine, is one of the fastest four-wheel-drive production cars of all time. Although its lofty appearance didn't suggest it could snap at the heels of Lamborghinis and Aston Martins, it could accelerate from standstill to 62mph in 4.5 seconds and reach a 180mph top speed.

The Range Rover fuse was probably lit by Rover's acquisition, in early 1965, of the rights to an all-aluminium 3.5-litre V8 engine design from General Motors in the USA. The power unit had been used in several Buick and Oldsmobile models in the early 1960s, but GM had abandoned it. The engine was first spotted by Rover managing director William Martin-Hurst on a visit to Mercury Marine in the USA, and he negotiated a deal to buy it in a few months, which even included GM engineer Joe Turley coming to the UK to help Rover manufacture a mildly updated version at Solihull. The engine was shortly installed in the P5 luxury saloon and the P6 executive car.

Its excellent performance and low weight (200lb less than the P5's old 3-litre, six-cylinder 'iron' engine) completely transformed both cars into Jaguar and Mercedes-Benz rivals.

The engine was ready-made for a kind of super-Land Rover too, still referred to as a Road-Rover, and in 1966 the long-gestating idea finally got the official green light from Rover bosses, and the full-time attention of top Rover engineers Gordon Bashford and Spencer King. At its heart the new car was, essentially, a compromise, the optimum combination of on- and off-road performance. Although a substantial separate chassis, similar to the box-section ladder-frame type used in Land Rovers, was a given, leaf-spring suspension was definitely out – the ride would be too harsh and uncomfortable – and suspension for the beam axles by low-rate coil springs was devised instead. This increased vertical wheel travel from the Land Rover's bone-shaking 4in to 10in on the new car, providing much better bump absorption, a consequently more forgiving ride, and wheels in contact with the ground for more of the time, for better stability.

It was obvious to the development team that permanent four-wheel drive was crucial. A selectable system like the Land Rover's was fine for an off-road vehicle in a limited environment; most of them worked hard but didn't go far.

But this new car would be driving fast over long distances, and the strain put on the components by switching from two- to four-wheel drive could be damaging. Tests showed a permanent system would also extend tyre life from 11,000 to 30,000 miles. The transmission was designed with a Salisbury Powr-Lok central differential, with limited-slip controlled by friction clutches inside it, and separate differentials for front and rear axles to synchronise speeds between left and right wheels. The centre diff had a lock to evenly spread power to each wheel if one or other lost traction or became jammed.

Rover's new V8 engine was a natural, particularly as it gave optimum torque – pulling power – at the lower end of its rev range. Splitting and distributing this torque evenly was another reason full-time four-wheel drive was called for. However, although the other Rover cars with V8 engines came only with automatic transmission to suit their luxury positioning in the car market, this all-new car would still need a manual gearbox to make it versatile in all conditions, and Land Rover's own four-speeder was adapted to fit. All-round disc brakes were fitted.

The wheelbase Bashford and King settled on measured 99.9in and so, not unnaturally, the car was formally known at this early stage as the 100in Station Wagon. Nevertheless, the 'Road-Rover' name still appeared

Noel Edmonds was invited to drive the 317,615th – and final – example of the original Range Rover off the production line on 15 February 1996. By his own reckoning Edmonds had already owned some fifty Range Rovers. In 1997, he spent £125,000 on a one-off model with CCTV, external camera monitors, a panic button, an early tracking system, internet access, and a screen for video conferencing.

on models taking shape in Rover's styling studios. There, head stylist David Bache, whose skilful hand had created both the P5 and P6, was brimming over with ideas for a radical-looking car to merge lofty off-roader with modern saloon. He aimed for a wedge-shaped fastback with unusual window lines, not dissimilar to a giant 1970s hatchback like a Volkswagen Golf. While Bache worked on this early concept, Spencer King had secretly 'borrowed' another member of the styling staff, Geoff Compton, for a couple of hours, and he'd quickly drawn up a basic 'mule' body design to fit around King's and Bashford's vehicle hardpoints, with plenty of King's own intuitive input. This enabled the engineering department to build themselves a basic body to complete a driveable prototype, and so press on with development at full tilt.

The styling department was frantically busy on other work anyway. But when the Rover board saw the fully built prototype they instantly fixated on the rightness of the King/Compton overall shape and, with time slipping by, Bache had to be cajoled into accepting the basic exterior design as it stood. Nonetheless, he insisted on being allowed to fettle it.

'The first two prototypes were designed for functionality rather than style and were called "clinker-built" because King had been

◀◀ With its body hastily built in 1967 to get the project underway, this '100-inch Station Wagon' was already broadly familiar as the final Range Rover. Photo courtesy Graham Robson.

inspired by boat building,' recalled Range Rover project engineer Geoff Miller. This gave a pair of bizarre, parallel creases, with slight shadows, running the length of the car. 'One of the clever things Bache did was to change the lower crease above the sill to an outward step, turning the lower shadow into a highlight. It made a big difference to the appearance of the vehicle.'

This secondary waistline, carried around and over the wheel arches, cleverly helped mask the car's visual bulk. Other changes Bache made included the front grille as a neat row of matching vertical slats, a re-profiled clamshell bonnet, prominent rectangular light clusters at the car's corners, and a black vinyl covering for the C-pillar to give the impression of a 'floating' roof. Concealed door handles and Rostyle-type wheels lent visual sophistication. It was a masterful exercise in finessing an already sound design – one where form really did follow function in the Land Rover tradition.

By the time the Road-Rover was handed over to Rover's proving department to be readied for production in late 1968, there was quiet confidence that it was a winner. It would be like nothing else on sale, and the combination of the board's vision, the go-anywhere Land Rover reputation, and the excellence of the new car's engineering added up to something really special.

Not, it should be said, that it was then regarded as a nascent status symbol, more a supremely competent dual-purpose estate car. Pondering on its success years later, King recalled: 'It was never intended to be a luxury car, it was a work vehicle for builders and farmers, but it was dragged up by customer demand.' The interior, therefore, was comfortable but hardwearing, with vinyl seats and rubber mats instead of carpets so that it could withstand muddy boots and wet dogs, and even being hosed out. The engine, undeniably powerful, was given a lower compression ratio so it could cope with low-grade petrol in

▼ Stylist David Bache's considered design proposal for the Road Rover was much more car-like – a real 'crossover'.

▼ A reproduction of the original clay model being demonstrated by engineer Roger Crathorne at 'The Range Rover Story' display at Solihull in 2017.

far-flung markets. The specification was full of touches intended to keep the car performing strongly even when in the most arduous conditions; for example, special baffles in the oil sump made sure the oil pump couldn't be starved on severe gradients. Specially adapted Stromberg carburettors were adopted, in place of Rover's customary SUs, for similar reasons of being able to keep working properly as the car was tilted at awkward angles when on the move off-road.

In 1966, just as the Road-Rover was coalescing, The Rover Company was taken over by the Leyland Motor Corporation; a couple of years later and the parent company became the British Leyland Motor Corporation after its merger with British Motor Holdings, the company consisting of the British Motor Corporation (Austin, MG, Morris, Riley and Wolseley) and Jaguar. The chairman of the massive new company, Sir Donald Stokes,

◄ This sturdy, coil-sprung chassis of one of the Velar prototypes on display at Solihull was driveable.

came along to Solihull early in '68, and was given a demonstration run in a Road-Rover prototype on the company's own cross-country test track, called 'The Jungle' by Rover engineer Tom Barton. He came back from this hair-raising experience hugely impressed. 'Press on with work on this British world-beater,' he declared. To that end, British Leyland registered a 'decoy' trademark in London, Velar, derived from the Italian verb *velare*, meaning to veil or cover-up. Using the name on seven engineering prototypes, twenty-seven pre-production cars and twenty press demonstration vehicles was a cunning ruse to disguise them, and confuse rivals, as the Road-Rover entered its final phase of prototype evaluation in the UK and on demanding terrain abroad. With such a sound and immensely capable basic design, now it was down to intensive detail work to, for instance, eliminate squeaks and rattles from the body –

Coachbuilder Wood & Pickett once built a limited-edition Range Rover sold exclusively through Harrods in Knightsbridge. In 1981, the store commissioned the car with roof rack (for shopping), alloy wheels, sloping and slatted grille, fancy interior and gauche paintwork in Harrods' trademark green and gold.

all aluminium, like a Land Rover, with steel bonnet and lower tailgate – and to make the interior fully water- and dust-proof. The Velars had many variations of detail in interior design as Rover fine-tuned the overall package in carefully calculated anticipation of the first customers. It was a constant struggle to control costs, so the car could go on sale at no more than £2,000. Any more, warned the company's marketing team, and it doubted many people would be tempted.

There was one, additional change: all thoughts of 100in Station Wagon, Road-Rover and Velar were banished when the decision was taken to call this dramatic vehicle the Range Rover.

◄ Spen King, father of the Range Rover, in a ghostly depiction at the 'Range Rover Story' show at Solihull.

On 17 June 1970, Rover's groundbreaking new car was revealed to the media. The location was the rugged and rocky area around the Blue Hills Mine in St Agnes, Cornwall. It was the perfect place to demonstrate the Range Rover's hitherto unheard-of dual personality, and the reception from the press was extremely positive.

One magazine dubbed it a 'go-anywhere estate car', as people grappled with the all-new concept. And while the launch price of £1,998 was some £200 beyond the cheapest Jaguar XJ6, and £2 more than the also brand-new Triumph Stag, the Range Rover was touted as a practical working vehicle that performed as well off the highway as on it. No leather seats, no hi-fi, no electric windows, and even a heated rear window cost extra. But there was nothing else like it, and the prominent capitals spelling out R-A-N-G-E R-O-V-E-R front and back reinforced the impression of confident new intent from Britain's most forward-looking carmaker.

As soon as they drove one, people were mightily impressed. In November 1970, motoring journalist Stuart Bladon devised a rigorous test route: the entire length of the M6 motorway which was then under construction near Birmingham and Coventry, and therefore offered both fresh tarmac and, as he said, 'seas of mud'. He wrote: 'On conclusion of the journey I was

▲ Snapshots of early Velar pre-production cars at the time of the Range Rover's unveiling in Cornwall in June 1970.

convinced that no other vehicle could have coped ... nothing else can set such a high overall standard for both sets of conditions.'

One of the most extravagant special versions of the original Range Rover was the 1980 Rapport Excelsior, with a 35in stretch to incorporate vast rear doors leading on to virtually a mobile throne room for wealthy Middle Eastern customers. With a faux-Rolls grille, and four round headlamps, a 4.4-litre version of Rover's V8 engine was needed to power it.

Then in January 1971 *Motor* magazine gave the Range Rover an unusually forensic road-test analysis over 2,200 miles. 'We're enormously impressed,' it gushed, before adding soberly, 'The absence of conspicuous sacrifice for versatility's sake is perhaps the car's greatest attraction.'

The magazine was fortunate to borrow the test car when there was plenty of rain and snow – ideal test conditions, then:

We tried the car through deep rutted mud and over rock beds and couldn't fault its performance. A short wheelbase also helps to clear sharp bumps and ridges. It is here that the car scores over the firmly sprung Land Rover. Inevitably there is plenty of body movement over really bad surfaces, but it is always well cushioned, never harsh, thumpy or spine-jarring.

But that was just the verdict off-road. *Motor* found its ride and handling over tarmac a revelation for something so large, while accepting a bit of body roll on sharp corners. It was awe-struck at its roadholding on snow and in sub-zero conditions. 'The remarkable 4wd traction greatly increased the safety margin on icy corners.' Not only that but with its smooth V8 power, the Range Rover accelerated faster than a Citroen DS21 to 60mph and could cruise comfortably at 85

RANGE ROVER MKI

On sale: 1970–96
Engine capacity, configuration: 3,528cc, 3,946cc & 4,275cc, V8 petrol; 2,393cc & 2,497cc, straight-four-cylinder turbodiesel
Body styles: two- or four-door estate with split tailgate
Dimensions: 4,470–4,653mm long, 1,780mm high, 1,780mm wide
wheelbase: 2,540–2,743mm
Top speed: 92–110mph
Sample acceleration figures: 3,528cc – 0–60mph in 12.9sec.; 4,275cc LSE – 0–60mph in 9.9sec.; 2,393cc turbodiesel – 0–60mph in 16.5sec.
Sample prices:
Range Rover in 1970 – £1,998
Vogue SE in 1988 – £27,349
Vogue LSE in 1994 – £40,899

▲ Motoring journalists are here amazed at the Range Rover's abilities at the 1970 press launch in Falmouth.

while just able to kiss 100. As *Motor* cheekily noted, 'Other drivers don't expect to be dusted off by what looks like a small bus.'

Even when fully loaded with five passengers and luggage, an ingeniously simple component kept the car level; this was the Boge Hydromat device at the back between the chassis and a centre point on the rear axle, which acted as a large extra damper progressively pumped up by axle movement.

Seats, driving position, dashboard (simply yet cunningly designed so it functioned unmodified with right- or left-hand drive) and heating all won lavish praise, and there was something else new in a relatively conventional car: spectacular all-round visibility; another feather in the Range Rover safety cap.

With, in effect, eight speeds from the high- and low-ratio sets, there was a gear for every possible sort of driving condition. However, the magazine's experts found the change slow and heavy, more like something from a lorry, and the transfer lever between ratios stiff. The steering was found to be heavy too, and responses on the move rather ponderous, so caution was urged for enthusiastic drivers used to normal cars. Oh, and the boxy Range Rover shape tended to draw road muck on to the rear window – it was crying out for a wiper and washer.

There was an immediate stampede to get one of the new Range Rovers.

▼ A Range Rover demonstrator makes short work of a steep Cornish hillside at the 1970 launch event.

➤ This is the very first press advertisement for the new Range Rover, one that tries to attune the buying public to a brand-new type of passenger car.

The cascade of orders guaranteed an immediate waiting list months long. For years, Range Rovers suffered virtually no depreciation and each time the car was launched in a new market there was dismay when the initial stock sold out immediately. The Solihull factory simply couldn't match the demand that was unleashed.

Indeed, the Range Rover was a rare bright spot in the first half of the 1970s for British Leyland, whose mainstream cars like the Austin Allegro and Morris Marina were cursed with problems. The reward the vehicle received for the brilliant way it was executed by the Rover team was to be deprived of funds to develop it. Apart from a change of Salisbury Powr-Lok diff to discard

◄ Clockwise from top left: it looks austere, but the original modular dashboard was an ingenious design easily adaptable to right- or left-hand drive; seatbelts were built into the front seats to allow easy access to the rear bench seat when tipped forward; plenty of cargo space when the rear seat was folded, with spare wheel tethered upright on the left; comfortable seating with a commanding driving position, although the abundant plastics were designed chiefly for easy maintenance.

the limited-slip function (it made the driveline uncomfortably stiff) after some 300 Range Rovers had been built, very little changed for years.

There was logic in leaving the car mostly unaltered for almost a decade. Rover was reluctant to add features to its fairly spartan specification to prevent Britain's rampant inflation from putting it beyond the means of customers. By 1973, for example, the price had doubled to over £4,000. But, mostly, British Leyland felt the Range Rover, like the Mini, looked after itself while the firefighting was done on other fronts.

It's astonishing to recall, though, that the same six paint colours offered at launch were still the only choices nine years later, and that despite the affluence of the Range Rover clientele, calls for luxury features fitted at the factory were ignored. Nonetheless, the very worthwhile option of power-assisted steering did arrive in 1973, along with a rear wash/wipe – and a cigarette lighter – as standard.

Restricted supplies, and the Range Rover's natural appeal to wealthy landowners, rapidly turned it into a status symbol, its lofty and commanding driving position well suited to upper-crust owners who felt most at home when at similar heights on horseback (towing a horsebox was easy meat for a Rangie). The practical comfort it offered was tasteful in precisely

➤➤ The Range Rover's brilliantly balanced styling was helped by door handles concealed in the edges of the two doors.

> Wealthy buyers were soon choosing a Range Rover as an alternative to a large family estate car.

> Rover's 3.5-litre V8 engine was a natural for the Range Rover because it was light – all-aluminium – and powerful.

the same way Hunter wellies or a Barbour jacket were. It won the RAC Dewar Trophy for 'Outstanding British technical achievement in the automotive world', and the Don Safety Trophy, both in 1971. Famously, its angular and well-balanced form earned it a temporary place in the Louvre in Paris as a piece of exemplary industrial design – that had never been bestowed on a Ferrari, Lamborghini or Porsche.

After British Leyland's bankruptcy and nationalisation in 1974–75, there was no money available to update the car whatsoever, and it continued to be built unchanged year after year while doing its bit to make Land Rover one of the few commercially viable parts

˅ The first Range Rover instantly became a true car design icon and set incredible new benchmarks in on/off-road ability.

▲ The drop-down lower tailgate was one of the first Range Rover's few steel panels and was therefore prone to rust.

of the stricken industrial empire. Finally, in 1978, Land Rover Ltd was separated out from the rest of the firm, and a new management team examined its allocated budget and – finally – considered ways to expand the Range Rover's already irresistible appeal.

The first, modest results were revealed in September 1979. As well as extra paint colours and matt black, polyurethane-covered bumpers, a new four-spoke steering wheel, and items like power steering, tinted glass, optional front seat headrests, brushed nylon upholstery, a heated rear window and inertia-reel seatbelts all became standard.

➤ Clockwise from right: the design team always saw the Range Rover as a working vehicle, and Britain's police forces agreed, with plenty of orders for this versatile vehicle; Birmingham company Spencer Abbott was one of many conversion specialists to transform the Range Rover into a high-speed ambulance; fitted as standard from 1973, the rear wash/wipe system proved essential to keep the rear screen clear of muck drawn to its sheer surface.

In the past, the desire for air conditioning had been met with various Heath Robinson-type arrangements, including roof-mounted box units, but now a neatly integrated system joined the factory option list. The other improvements gave the Range Rover a long-overdue refresh, the air-con did the same for the well-heeled occupants.

◀ A Range Rover body unit about to be attached to its chassis on the Solihull production line.

▲ Carmichael added an extra set of wheels for its Range Rover-based fire engine called the Commando, popular with smaller airfields.

◄ Pictured in action in 1973, this left-hand-drive Range Rover would be one of thousands exported to meet seemingly insatiable worldwide demand.

▲ A 1976 Range Rover demonstrating its incredible contortions on an obstacle course at Rover's Gaydon test centre in Warwickshire.

▲ A modified Range Rover hard at work at Rover's Gaydon test track, showing how test data was gathered in those pre-digital days ...

◄◄ Clockwise from top left: This four-door conversion was available for export to special order from London coachbuilder FLM Panelcraft, with discreet backing from the Rover factory; reflecting the fact there was still nothing else like it, in 1978 the Range Rover was still a favourite with emergency services; the 1980 Range Rover, now with black polyurethane-covered bumpers, brought a host of long-overdue enhancements.

Why was there no four-door Range Rover? That had been a thorny issue since even before the original two-door was made public. For one thing, engineering a steel skeleton frame to adequately support rear passenger doors would have been costly, and a large sum had already been spent on designing seatbelts that were anchored to the front seats, not the B-pillars, so rear passengers could access the back seats – through the wide front doors – without getting tangled up in them.

A four-door configuration, though, would be far more practical. Rover built just such a prototype in 1972 but was denied the development budget to take it any further.

The resourceful company had long worked with trusted outside contractors, though, and if overseas customers really pressed for rear passenger doors (and remember that throughout the whole of the 1970s there were no European Range Rover rivals) then a neat conversion by London coachbuilder FLM Panelcraft received discreet backing from Solihull headquarters.

However, Swiss firm Monteverdi came up with an even better four-door rendition in 1980, slotting both side doors within the existing wheelbase, and with wind-down windows at the back and Morris Marina 'flap' door handles, which looked remarkably good within the Range Rover's starched overall lines.

With a newfound can-do attitude, a deal was quickly tied up with Monteverdi, at first offering the very expensive conversion through the Land Rover dealer network, and then from April 1981 building it in-house at Solihull. It was spectacularly successful; within a few months it accounted for 70 per cent of orders. The ingenuity of the four-door design even won a British Design Council award in 1982.

That year saw a raft of additional changes to make the interior more welcoming, including a lockable storage box between the front seats, extra carpeting and sound-deadening, door-mounted loudspeakers and full wiring to accept the owner's choice of hi-fi,

and more rear legroom by shifting the seat squab back, at the slight expense of cargo space.

The Range Rover was now easier to access and more relaxing to drive. The next priority was to dial

⋀ A six-wheeled Range Rover airport crash tender with four doors in service with the RAF, c.1985.

▼ Prestige and luxury came to the Range Rover for the first time in 1981, with this 'In Vogue' edition as a collaboration with the legendary fashion magazine.

in some opulence. And, once again, Land Rover chose to draw on the work of an independent company whose livelihood was Range Rover-dependent. In this case, it was London-based customisers Wood

▼ Prestige and luxury came to the Range Rover for the first time in 1981, with this 'In Vogue' edition as a collaboration with the legendary fashion magazine.

& Pickett, famous for its coach-built luxury Minis in the 1960s and now creating bespoke Range Rovers for clients in the UK and abroad, the Middle East especially.

Land Rover had collaborated with the fashionistas at *Vogue* magazine to create a one-off car for a promotion in the glossy magazine's pages. The most obvious identifying feature was the striking metallic Vogue Blue paintwork, but there were also walnut door cappings, stainless-steel tailgate trim, alloy wheels and a specially designed picnic hamper for the interior. The excellent reception afforded to the 'In Vogue' led Land Rover to work with Wood & Pickett to build a limited edition of the car

▲ An automatic gearbox was first offered in 1982, by which time all Range Rovers came with this four-spoke steering wheel.

▼ A brochure for the Carbodies Unitruck, which turned the Range Rover into a dual-purpose pick-up for hard work, and that could even include crop-spraying.

priced at £13,788. The hefty sticker price proved no off-put. With 700 examples made, all equipped with air conditioning and plenty of deep carpeting, twice as many were sold than originally planned. Clearly,

enormous untapped demand existed for a luxurious Range Rover, and two further In Vogue limited runs were marketed until a Vogue edition joined the standard model line-up with its own silver-grey cloth upholstery, alloy wheels and a four-speaker stereo radio-cassette player.

Aside from the cosmetic niceties, Land Rover engineers worked hard to improve the on-road driving experience. First came an optional Fairey overdrive for the four-speed gearbox, for more relaxed long-distance driving. Then in 1982 a five-speed gearbox arrived, the LT77 unit already used in British Leyland cars like the Rover SD1 and Triumph TR7. It gave a 10 per cent improvement in fuel consumption and a welcome

OPEN UP TO THE POSSIBILITIES OF Unitruck

The Multi-Purpose Work & Play Vehicle From Carbodies Of Coventry

◄ Clockwise from left: making a splash in the 1985 Vogue four-door, complete with new front air dam and fog lights; four doors finally arrived on the Range Rover in 1982, adopting a Swiss design – this is the 1985 Vogue model, clearly not stumped by anything; among the many unusual conversions offered by outside companies was this 1980 convertible from London's Rapport, complete with sloping bonnet and a Ford Granada grille.

25 per cent boost in fourth-gear acceleration times as that ratio had been lowered.

Lots of people yearned for a Range Rover; only a small number could actually afford one. In the late 1970s, however, there were still virtually no near-equivalents. At the budget end of the market, the 1977 Matra Rancho offered some of its high-riding style and a split tailgate, but with front-wheel drive its off-road capability was limited, even if running costs were very low. The Mercedes-Benz G-Wagen, introduced in 1979, had the kudos of a luxury brand but in those days was rather more akin to the Land Rover in terms of utility, even if like the Range Rover it rode on coil-spring suspension. In 1983, *Motor* magazine pitted a £15,642 four-door Range Rover against the

A Range Rover driven by Frenchmen Alain Génestier, Joseph Terbiaut and Jean Lemordant was the first car home on the very first Paris–Dakar rally in 1979. Scottish ex-racing driver and team owner Tom Walkinshaw prepared the Range Rover that won the 1981 event with Rene Metge and Robert Giroux driving.

▼ This elongated beast is the Rapport Excelsior of 1980, which needed a 4.4-litre Rover V8 to haul its 35in of extra metal, usually across the Middle East.

▲ London customisers Wood & Pickett built this special Range Rover for sale through Knightsbridge department store Harrods in 1982.

top-of-the-range £15,460 Mercedes-Benz 280GE, both automatics, and despite the Merc's formidable performance off-road, the tester still favoured the Range Rover. It wrote: 'Even with a three-pointed star on its grille, G-Wagen cannot challenge the refinement and style that are the keynotes of the Range Rover's long-standing success … Its crown remains firmly in place.'

Other manufacturers eyed up the esteem in which the Range Rover was held, and the latent desire to own one that many people nursed. Companies like Jeep, Nissan and

▲ The two impressive Popemobiles built for the Pontiff's UK visit in 1982 by Ogle Design, with the Leyland truck-based example dwarfing the already lofty Range Rover.

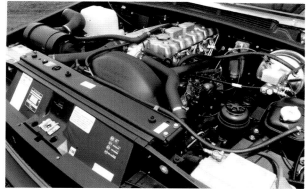

Toyota all offered proven four-wheel drive vehicles, but, for many, they were simply too agricultural and tiring to use every day. It was left to Mitsubishi with its 1982 Pajero/Shogun to create the first four-wheel-drive off-roader to offer similar levels of civilisation to the British standard-bearer at a more affordable price and with an economical 2.6-litre four-cylinder engine; a year later came a five-door model that offered similar proportions. Starting at £9,449 – two-thirds of the Range Rover's price – the Pajero was good value, well built, and blazed a trail for an explosion of new, lower-priced

▲ In 1982 Mitsubishi launched its Pajero (Shogun in the UK) off-roader, the first credible Range Rover rival to substantially undercut its big-ticket price; a four-cylinder turbocharged engine from Italy's VM Motori brought diesel power, and sloth, to the Range Rover for the first time in 1986.

➤➤ This Range Rover Turbo D, nicknamed the Beaver Bullet, set twenty-seven speed and endurance records; here it is doing just that at the Motor Industry Research Association test track in Nuneaton in August 1986.

Range Rover rivals as the 'sport-utility vehicle' sector gathered pace. In 1984, an even more significant rival emerged, the new Jeep Cherokee, with its chassis-less construction guaranteeing far more car-like handling responses, and safer on-road handling. In 1988, a very significant new player arrived: the first compact SUV, the Suzuki Vitara. Land Rover's own mass-market 4x4 passenger car, the Discovery, was launched a year later.

Sales of the Range Rover increased strongly throughout the 1980s as, each year, dozens of small improvements and refinements were carried out. The Vogue SE model arrived in 1986, equipped with electronic fuel-injection, and within two years the standard specification included full leather upholstery, an electric sunroof, metallic paint and alloy wheels matched to the body colour. Anti-lock brakes arrived in 1989 – a first on an SUV – followed by a bigger-capacity 3.9-litre engine in 1990. In 1987 the Range Rover finally arrived in the USA, where the ever more extravagant spec established it firmly as a pukka luxury product.

Nevertheless, 'working' Range Rovers weren't overlooked. A fairly basic Fleetline model was available from 1981 to '85, and in 1986 a new turbodiesel option joined the line-up, with a 2.4-litre (2.5 from 1990, with improved low-down torque)

▲ 1980s Range Rover owners were, naturally, users of the first mobile phones; here's a particularly bulky Ericsson model in a scene of period yuppie bliss.

these cars nicknamed the 'Beaver Bullet' set twenty-seven sprint and endurance records for diesel cars in 1986, including becoming the first ever to maintain an average speed of over 100mph for twenty-four hours during three days' slog at the MIRA test track in Nuneaton. After 1986, the two-door model was for export only, apart from the desirable 1991 limited-edition CSK, of which 200 were built to celebrate the esteemed Range Rover creator Charles Spencer King.

King, who died in 2010, always remained a little irritated that his phenomenally capable Range Rover came to be considered as a rich man's plaything. But in 1992 came factory acknowledgement that a

four-cylinder engine from Italy's VM Motori (after a diesel-ised version of the V8 engine was considered and rejected). It was slow and relatively unrefined but could manage 26mpg in everyday driving. One of

Range Rover was indeed now an alternative to a luxury limousine like a Mercedes-Benz S-class or Lexus LS400. It was in the form of the new LSE model with a wheelbase lengthened by 8in to provide significantly more rear legroom. Happily, the evergreen looks of the Range Rover weren't harmed at all by this stretch. Below the surface, moreover, was an all-new air suspension system known as ECAS (Electronically Controlled Air Suspension). Removing the steel springs permitted a variable ride height which, when at its lowest setting, made the LSE a much more stable car at speeds over 50mph. At rest, it also made the car easier to load up with cargo.

Electronic traction control was also incorporated for the first time on any off-roader.

Mature and much loved, the Range Rover was getting long in the tooth by the time its replacement arrived in 1994. However, there was still an

▾ This enormous Range Rover special by Cartel, called the Surrey Six, was said to be the ultimate ever Range Rover when it was unveiled in 1984.

➤ Clockwise from top left: a Range Rover Tdi from around 1992 with the kind of passenger you'd expect in the favourite car of the hunting/shooting/fishing brigade; this highly desirable two-door limited edition of 1991, the CSK, was built to salute the always-modest Charles Spencer King, one of the Range Rover's key designers; the long-wheelbase Vogue LSE (left) facing the standard Vogue SE in 1992.

overlap of two years. This was partly to ensure everyone anywhere in the world who could possibly want a 'Range Rover Classic' had a chance to order one, and partly to allow the new car to bed down at Solihull until the inevitable teething troubles were ironed out.

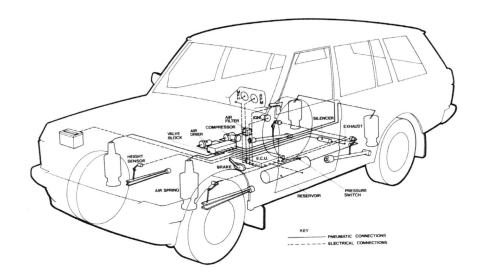

AIR FILTER

ICM

IGN.

SILENCER

EXHAUST

VALVE BLOCK

AIR DRIER

COMPRESSOR

HEIGHT SENSOR

BRAKE

E.C.U.

AIR SPRING

PRESSURE SWITCH

RESERVOIR

KEY
—————— PNEUMATIC CONNECTIONS
– – – – – – ELECTRICAL CONNECTIONS

◄ The LSE's air-suspension system was designed to make the Range Rover more of a ground-hugger on the road, and easier to climb into when stationary.

➤ The lengthened wheelbase of the LSE provided exceptionally generous rear legroom.

➤ TV presenter and long-time Range Rover addict Noel Edmonds drove the final Range Rover 'Classic' off the line on 15 February 1996.

The second-generation Range Rover Sport was introduced in 2013. It was now a derivative of the range-topping Range Rover, sharing a completely aluminium monocoque structure, rather than the slightly smaller Discovery. The car was launched by James Bond actor Daniel Craig in New York.

A late-model Range Rover; after more than two decades it was still one of the most desirable new cars on sale.

RANGE ROVER

L205 WNJ

When BMW made its shock acquisition of the Rover Group in 1994, it was already familiar with the new Range Rover. The German company was supplying its own straight-six 2.5-litre turbodiesel engine for the car that, by necessity, had been developed by Land Rover on a relatively tiny £300m shoestring. In 1988, the British government sold Rover Group to British Aerospace, using its favoured military contractor for the politically sensitive task of returning the carmaker – formerly the notorious British Leyland – to the private sector. During its short tenure, budgets were tightly restricted, which meant the new Rangie was, in effect, a rebody of the long-wheelbase Classic. As ever with Land Rover, there were several codenames for the car, including Pegasus and P38A ... the name of the modest building within Solihull housing the development team!

Technically, the car adopted the LSE's electronic suspension system across the whole range, incorporated into an 18 per cent stiffer version of the existing ladder-frame chassis, along with standard anti-lock brakes. The five suspension heights available, lowest to highest, spoke for themselves: Access, Motorway, Standard, Off-Road, and Off-Road Extended. Although the BMW turbodiesel was new, the venerable Rover V8 thundered on, now offered in 190bhp 4.0-litre

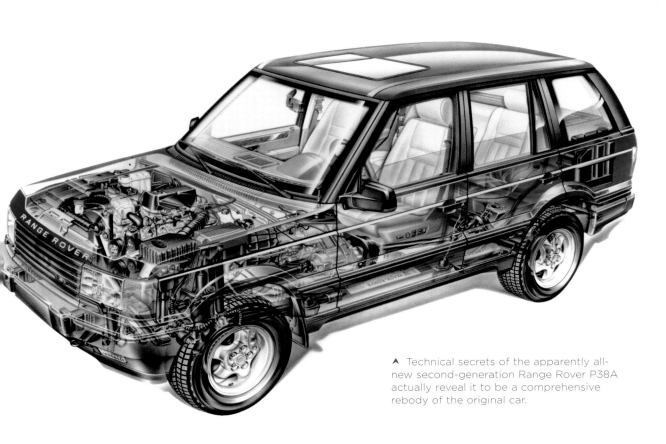

▲ Technical secrets of the apparently all-
new second-generation Range Rover P38A
actually reveal it to be a comprehensive
rebody of the original car.

and 225bhp 4.6-litre iterations and benefiting from the BMW/Bosch engine-management system already well proven in the BMW 7-series. Transmission choice included five-speed manual and four-speed automatic.

The car was launched in September 1994. It was a bit of an anti-climax, frankly. The new styling was underwhelming. It was neat enough, executed by Land Rover design chief George Thomson. But that was the problem. The original had such character, and this evolution had rather taken the crisp distinctiveness away. While the tall glasshouse, the apparently floating roof and the clamshell bonnet remained, the way they were drawn together looked bland, not helped by the derivative and prominent oblong headlights replacing the distinctive round ones. Admittedly, Land Rover had done lots of customer market research, and the result called for a conservative approach. Still, with a drag coefficient of 0.38, at least it was significantly more aerodynamic.

➤ The 4-litre V8 version of the new car doing its off-road stuff; there was no doubting its immense capability.

Clockwise from top left: cavernous boot-space and an asymmetrically split rear seat; this is the 2.5 DSE model: produced on a comparatively tiny budget and improved in most key areas, many still found the new styling underwhelming; the 2.5 DSE again here; BMW's excellent 2.5-litre six-cylinder turbodiesel was a key upgrade for the MkII Range Rover.

The first ever petrol-electric hybrid Range Rover was introduced in 2016, yoking electric power for town work to a 3-litre V6 turbodiesel engine for sustained all-day motorway driving. For the 2019 model year, however, a plug-in electric drivetrain was introduced on the P400e version, using the much smaller 2.0-litre Ingenium engine along with an 85kw electric motor. The headline statistic was emissions of just 72g/km.

RANGE ROVER MKII (P38A)

On sale: 1994–2002
Engine capacity, configuration: 3,946cc & 4,552cc, V8 petrol; 2,497cc, straight-six turbodiesel
Body style: four-door estate with split tailgate
Dimensions: 4,712mm long, 1,890mm high, 1,819mm wide; wheelbase: 2,746mm
Top speed: 101–119mph
Sample acceleration figures: 2,497cc turbodiesel – 0–60mph in 14.3sec.; 4,552cc V8 – 0–60mph in 9.6sec.
Sample price: Range Rover HSE in 1994 – £43,950

Inside, an entirely new dash was a step-up in fit and finish, with a particularly stylish curved centre console. With BMW in charge from just prior to the car's public launch, though, there were new quality standards to meet, and the Germans evidently found Solihull's build quality wanting. Out in the market, buyers were often frustrated by the unreliability of the increased onboard electronics. With the generally lukewarm reception, though, BMW soon decided to pour all its efforts into a totally new, third-generation car, and let the MkII model fulfil an interim role. Hence a plan to substitute the ageing Rover engines

▲ Left: the extremely comfortable cabin of the top-of-the-range 4.6 HSE.

Right: enlarged 4.6-litre version of Rover's faithful V8 engine would be the biggest ever offered as standard in a Range Rover.

▲ Left: a 1999 Autobiography treatment for the Range Rover could produce any kind of ambience the wealthy owner demanded.
Right: a 2001 Autobiography makeover for the neat and stylish basic dashboard of a MkII Range Rover.

with BMW's own V8s was deferred, and thoughts about a BMW V12-powered 'supercar' edition were dropped altogether.

Instead, the P38A Range Rover received a mid-life revamp in an urgent push to boost quality and choice. In 1995 the Autobiography personalisation programme was introduced for the 4.0SE and 4.6HSE, with inexhaustible combinations of non-standard paintwork, leather upholstery and wood trim. A year later the choice extended to a vast roster of in-car entertainment options and then, in 1997, the first satellite navigation system. From September 1998 there was regularly a Vogue SE edition among the line-up, groaning with equipment, and the final one cost an eye-popping £57,995, complete with its integral TV and video package. It sold very strongly, as it was an extremely capable vehicle no matter how people grumbled about its looks: 167,041 found buyers.

▲ The 30th anniversary edition of the P38A Rangie, of which 100 cars were built in 2000, finished in Wimbledon green.

Supermodel Kate Moss was being driven to a fashion shoot on 6 September 2000 when her Range Rover collided with a car on the A13 near Basildon, Essex. Both cars left the road and careered down an embankment. Moss was immediately airlifted to Basildon Hospital with a suspected shoulder injury, while her driver and two other people had to make do with an ambulance. She sustained only bruises, but the shoot was cancelled.

▲ This exclusive special edition was produced in association with shotgun maker Holland & Holland.

◄ Anti-lock brakes and five suspension-height settings were key features of the P38A Range Rover, here in 4-litre V8 form.

▲ The P38A was a very successful car, selling strongly everywhere, as with this example in Italy.

▲ The very last of the P38As leaves the production line, with Spen King in the passenger seat as the era of his world-famous design finally ended.

BMW started with a totally clean slate for replacing the Range Rover with a car it considered worthy of the illustrious name and set to work in 1995 while the P38A was still box-fresh. This time nothing would be carried over from the marque's historical roots. It would have a brand-new structure with brand-new engines.

The most radical thing about the car, codenamed L322, was underneath. The substantial separate chassis and beam axles had served three decades of Range Rover brilliantly, but, as the new millennium beckoned, it was obvious they'd reached the absolute limits of what could be expected of them for refining out noise, vibration and harshness where it mattered most: on the road.

So, this new Range Rover had unitary construction, but, thanks to a reworked, fully-independent air-suspension set-up (the first ever in a full-sized SUV), it retained the same wheel articulation that had always given the car such exceptional rock-hopping ability. At 113in, the wheelbase was longer than before, which helped the overall larger proportions of the all-new body. Masterminded by design chief Geoff Upex and lead designer Don Myatt – after an intense internal competition including proposals from BMW itself and several Italian studios – this time the new look hit the target bang-on – a skilful amalgam of the crispness of the original with raked-back modernity. Circular double-headlight styling was back in a bold, imposing frontage, while the double-slatted vents in the front wings looked like nothing else and paid homage to the concealed door handles in the edges of the doors on the original. The Range Rover was back on form.

Under the new bonnet, its clamshell profile carefully preserved, the Rover motor had finally been usurped by BMW's M62-type 4.4-litre V8 engine with 286bhp and 325lb ft of torque for both urge and pulling power, with a 3.0-litre M57 BMW turbodiesel as a less fuel-heavy option (and with more torque at lower revs). There were no longer any manual gearboxes, with five-speed ZF automatics only.

RANGE ROVER MKIII (L322)

On sale: 2002–12
Engine capacity, configuration: 4,197cc, 4,394cc, 4,398cc & 4,999cc, V8 petrol; 2,926cc, straight-six turbodiesel; 3,630cc & 4,367cc, V8 turbodiesel
Body style: four-door estate with split tailgate
Dimensions: 4,950–4,976mm long, 1,862–1,877mm high, 1,923mm wide; wheelbase: 2,800mm
Top speed: 110–140mph
Sample acceleration figures: 3,630cc V8 turbodiesel – 0–62mph in 9.2sec.; 4,999cc V8 supercharged – 0–62mph 6.2sec.
Sample price: Range Rover Vogue 4.4-litre petrol in 2003 – £59,995

By the time the new Rangie was unveiled in 2001, ownership of the marque had, almost unbelievably, changed once again. BMW broke up the Rover Group in 2000, keeping the Mini and the Cowley factory for itself, unloading the Rover cars business and Longbridge plant to its management, and selling Land Rover, Range Rover included, to Ford for £1.8 billion.

Consequently, just as soon as it could, Land Rover re-plumbed the Range Rover to release it from the costly obligation to use BMW's engines. In 2005 they were replaced by Jaguar petrol engines in the form of the AJ-V8 in 4.2-litre form with supercharger at 400bhp and 4.4-litre normally aspirated form at 306bhp; a year later and BMW's turbodiesel was ousted by Ford's super-torquey 3.6-litre TDV8. Satisfyingly, all the engines were now British-made once again. By 2010, the engine line-up had been revised once more to a 5.0-litre petrol engine with and without supercharger, and a twin-turbo 4.4-litre diesel.

It often takes an outsider to recognise the scope in something local, and it certainly seemed like Ford had realised the true potential of Range Rover within its portfolio of upmarket names now stabled together in its Premier Automotive Group. Land Rover had massively expanded its range, first with the Discovery in 1989 and then the compact Freelander in 1997, and

>> The BMW-instigated L322 Range Rover was new throughout, based around a monocoque body/chassis unit with all-independent air suspension.

▾ Designer Geoff Upex led the British team that created the third-generation Range Rover, beating Italian design studios that tendered for the job.

now vehicles (the bedrock, old-style Defender aside) were being replaced every few years, rather than every few decades. Apart from Jeep, it was the only automotive marque dedicated to four-wheel drive off-road passenger vehicles,

and it offered them to suit almost every pocket. Now it began using the Range Rover magic to ramp things up as, in 2004, the wraps came off the Range Rover Sport.

Superficially it resembled the top-of-the-pile Range Rover given a lower, sportier roofline. Yet the Sport was actually based on the Discovery 3 and so was rather more compact. A similar range of V8 petrol engines to those in the Range Rover were offered, although initially with a 2.7-litre V6 turbodiesel, but it shared its innovative Terrain Response system – which let the driver adjust the transmission and chassis settings for off-road conditions from grass to gravel and from snow to rocks. The Range Rover Sport also came

▲ Left: it may have dispensed with a separate chassis, but the all-new Range Rover was still pretty much unrivalled for its on/off-road compromise.

Right: the circular headlight theme of the original car was restored, and the castellated clamshell bonnet remained a key design feature.

with a standard centre e-diff that electronically locked and unlocked to apportion torque via a multi-plate clutch inside the transfer case. Meanwhile, an in-dash display could relay such information as steering angle and whether a wheel had lost contact with the ground.

RANGE ROVER SPORT MKI

On sale: 2004–13
Engine capacity, configuration: 4,196cc, 4,394cc & 4,999cc, V8 petrol; 2,720cc, 2,993cc & 3,630cc, V6 turbodiesel
Body style: five-door estate
Dimensions: 4,737–4,783mm long, 1,605–1,816mm high, 1,928–1,933mm wide; wheelbase 2,745mm
Top speed: 120–155mph
Sample acceleration figure: 4,999cc V8 petrol supercharged – 0–60mph in 6.0sec.
Sample price: 2.7 TDV6 SE five-door auto in 2005 – £42,355

◀ The L322 Range Rover being assembled at a Solihull plant that saw huge investment from BMW for the task.

The Range Rover contributes some £10 billion to the UK economy annually, constituting its biggest single 'luxury' export product. Range Rover makes up 85 per cent of all the luxury cars built in the UK. At Solihull alone, 10,000 people work on the cars, and 44 per cent of everything JLR makes is Range Rovers.

▲ The sumptuous interior of the L322 Range Rover, in this case a 2007 model year car.

▲ The Autobiography edition of the Range Rover in 2009, with Aniline leather upholstery and plentiful wood accents.

◄ Much of the crisp, individualistic style of the original Range Rover had been restored for the brand-new car in 2002.

◄◄ A fleeting 2010 Range Rover; by this time the car had switched entirely to British-made engines, and Land Rover was owned by Tata Motors.

◄ The stylish 2004 Range Rover Sport shared its underpinnings with the Land Rover Discovery.

➤ With a 5-litre supercharged V8 engine, the Range Rover Sport was very fast indeed, and had to be limited to 155mph.

➤ The Sport brought the Range Rover kudos to an ever-wider audience, with excellent off-road credentials.

Richard Branson has been a keen Range Rover owner. When motoring along the M40 in 1994 with his family, his example unexpectedly went out of control, vaulting the central reservation and ending up on its roof. They all walked away unscathed and Virgin Atlantic later ordered a fleet of Range Rover courtesy cars.

◄ A Range Rover Sport crossing the Mekong River (with a little human help) as the brand pushed into the Chinese market.

The Range Rover Sport was a huge hit, but it was just a prelude to the next extension of the Range Rover theme in 2010, when the Evoque arrived at the Paris motor show. The high-riding, big-wheeled, wedge-shaped look of the car, with its bulging wheel arches and narrow side-window line, were familiar from the Land Rover LRX concept car, first shown in 2008. They were overseen by long-time Land Rover design chief Gerry McGovern. The unexpected aspects of the Evoque were that it put this showpiece on the road in barely altered visual form, and that it carried the Range Rover name down into the hugely wider compact SUV sector. Plus, it was acknowledged Evoque owners would probably go off-road only occasionally, despite some component-sharing with the rufty-tufty Freelander. For buyers who knew they'd never even do that, there was now (be it whispered in solemn-faced, traditionalist Land Rover circles) a two-wheel drive version, with front-wheel drive only.

Nonetheless, for those few-and-far-between forays into the rough, the Evoque was remarkably capable, with higher ground clearance even than its Freelander cousin, so it could drive through water half-a-metre deep, and the best take-off, departure and ramp angles of any similar rival, so it could take bumpy ground and steeper gradients literally in its stride. Moreover, Land Rover Hill Descent Control was an option, a system that automatically applied braking as the car was navigating a tricky downward slope.

The choice was extremely wide, with Ford EcoBoost 2-litre 237bhp petrol and two 2.2-litre 148/187bhp Duratorq turbodiesels (the lower-powered one for the 2WD car), six-speed manual or five-speed automatic transmission, and four trim-level packages. With the rest of the option and personalisation lists thrown in, there were said to be 380,000 types of Evoque theoretically available. But away from the marketing roster, this was an innovative car on its own:

lightweight construction was down to aluminium bonnet and roof, plastic front wings and composite tailgate (single-piece, despite Range Rover traditions, to keep

RANGE ROVER EVOQUE

On sale: 2011–19
Engine capacity, configuration: 1,999cc, straight-four petrol; 1,999–2,179cc, straight-four turbodiesel
Body styles: three-door hatchback; five-door hatchback, two-door convertible
Dimensions: 4,371mm long, 1,605–1,635mm high, 1,900mm wide; wheelbase: 2,660mm
Top speed: 113–134mph
Sample acceleration figures: 1,999cc turbodiesel – 0–60mph in 9.5sec.
Sample prices: Evoque 2.0 Si4 HSE Dynamic five-door auto in 2013 – £43,690

With a New York backdrop, the radical Land Rover LRX concept car was revealed in 2008.

weight low), while iron filings in the shock absorber fluid could be electrified to stiffen or soften the ride quality. Power steering was electronic while additional gadgetry could include a parking-assistance system and an 8in sat-nav screen.

In 2008, in a major change of strategy, Ford had sold both its Land Rover and Jaguar divisions to India's Tata Motors, which immediately formed Jaguar Land Rover (JLR) as its British-based prestige-car subsidiary. With the move came a switch in ownership of the former Ford plant at Halewood to the new entity. The Land Rover Freelander was already being produced there; now the related Range Rover Evoque joined it, and

soon after manufacture began on 4 July 2011 the Merseyside factory was working round the clock to satisfy Evoque demand. An amazing 80,000 examples were built in the first year, and after four years it

▼ Gerry McGovern, overlord of the modern Range Rover design ethos, with the 2008 LRX concept.

▲ The LRX, with its fully glazed roof and four individual seats, was even more startling on the inside.

▲ The Range Rover Evoque caused a sensation when it was unveiled in 2011, bringing the Range Rover name into direct conflict with other compact 'crossover' SUVs.

reached the half-million milestone. Eventually, assembly in Brazil, India and China was required to help Halewood meet demand.

The original three-door car was swiftly joined by a five-door stablemate, and then in 2016 came a four-seater convertible model with a conventional boot lid to replace the hatchback, and an electrically operated fabric top. At the same time, JLR's own Ingenium four-cylinder petrol and diesel engines replaced Ford's units.

Five doors made the Evoque much more practical and helped fuel enormous demand for the new small Range Rover.

▲ Workers at the Halewood factory on Merseyside had to toil round the clock to meet demand for the Evoque.

▲ An Evoque on the taxing Land Rover Experience at the jungle-like, off-road test circuit at the Solihull plant.

➤➤ The neat resolution of the Evoque's rear end, with bulging wheel arches and a narrow window line all round the car.

⋏ Land Rover's next bold move was to launch the first-ever convertible SUV, a soft-top Range Rover Evoque, here undergoing pre-sale off-road testing.

❥ Half a metre of water was no problem for an Evoque, and here a convertible is getting the most from the coast.

Congratulations Halewood on the 500,000 Range Rover Evoque

The fastest selling Land Rover in our history

◄◄ A top-hinged lid allowed decent luggage space inside the Evoque convertible's boot.

◄ In just four years, workers at Halewood produced half a million Evoques, making it one of Britain's most successful automotive products.

◄◄ A full-length glass roof panel was one of numerous options that could be specified, meaning very few Evoques turned out exactly the same.

◄ The sleek interior of an Evoque Dynamic with a Verve design theme.

Aluminium had long been recognised as a brilliant way to reduce weight in the construction of cars. It was, of course, the material for the original Land Rover's body panels back in 1948, and the shell for the first Range Rover in 1970. But well into the new century, aluminium alloy was also seen as key to lowering the industrial impact on the environment, by boosting fuel efficiency and recyclability.

The all-new 2012 Range Rover – the top-of-the-range flagship – therefore took a giant stride forward in aluminium usage. Its entire monocoque frame structure was made from it, an absolute first for any sport-utility vehicle, which resulted in a phenomenal 420kg being shorn from the 2,580kg heft of the outgoing car. A choice of wheelbases and engines, now including a V6 petrol-electric hybrid, was a world away from the basic single model that introduced the Range Rover forty-two years before, although the permanent four-wheel drive remained as probably the best off-road tool it was possible to buy in an ultra-luxurious car. A new system called All-Terrain Progress Control (ATPC) provided, in effect, an off-road cruise control for autonomous monitoring of speed from 1 to 19mph on all types of hostile terrain. Boosting the sumptuousness of the Range Rover was the SV Autobiography edition of 2015, with its sultry brushed-aluminium details, unique colour range and opulent executive seating.

Until 2017, the Velar name had been a footnote in the Range Rover's lengthening history – the secret codename used in 1968 to distract nosey parkers while Land Rover's '100in Station Wagon' was having its final shakedown on test tracks and public highways before it was revealed as the Range Rover in Cornwall in June 1970. Now, though, it had been plucked from obscurity to front the fourth Range Rover line.

RANGE ROVER MKIV (L405)

On sale: 2012–now
Engine capacity, configuration: 2,995cc, V6 petrol; 4,999cc, V8 petrol; 2,993cc, V6 turbodiesel; 4,367cc, V8 turbodiesel; 1,999cc, straight-four petrol/electric hybrid
Body style: four-door estate with split tailgate
Dimensions: 4,999–5,199mm long, 1,835mm high, 1,984mm wide; wheelbase: 2,922–3,122mm
Top speed: 130–155mph
Sample acceleration figures: 2,993cc V6 turbodiesel – 0–60mph in 7.1sec.; 4,999cc V8 supercharged – 0–60mph 6.5sec.
Sample price: Range Rover Vogue 4.4-litre turbodiesel in 2013 – £78,095

RANGE ROVER SPORT MKII

On sale: 2014–now.
Engine capacity, configuration:
1,999cc straight-four petrol;
2,995cc V6 petrol; 4,999cc V8 petrol;
2,993cc V6 turbodiesel; 4,367cc,
V8 turbodiesel; 1,999cc straight-four
petrol/electric hybrid
Body style: five-door estate
Dimensions: 4,851mm long,
1,811mm high, 2,073mm wide;
wheelbase: 2,923mm
Top speed: 136–162mph
Sample acceleration figure:
SVR 4,999cc V8 petrol supercharged
– 0–60mph in 4.5sec.
Sample price: HSE five-door auto
in 2018 – £64,085

RANGE ROVER VELAR

On sale: 2018–now
Engine capacity, configuration:
1,999cc straight-four petrol; 2,995cc
V6 petrol; 4,999cc V8 petrol; 2,993cc
V6 turbodiesel; 4,367c,
V8 turbodiesel
Body style: five-door estate.
Dimensions: 4,803mm long,
1,665mm high, 2,032mm wide;
wheelbase: 2,874mm
Top speed: 125–150mph
Sample acceleration figure:
R Dynamic HSE 2,995cc V6 petrol –
0–60mph in 5.3sec.
Sample price: Velar S 2.0 petrol
in 2018 – £50,930

➤➤ In 2010 the
next all-new Range
Rover took its bow,
becoming the first
SUV ever with an all-
aluminium structure.

▲ With plenty of power, and notwithstanding its ritzy image, the L405 upheld the legendary Range Rover towing prowess.

◄ The sumptuous new cabin of the 2012 car was the last word in luxury, and passenger entertainment.

In a way, the Range Rover Velar took the place of the Range Rover Sport in Land Rover's line-up; that one was now allied to the main Range Rover as a more compact, sportier alternative. Still, the Velar was a Range Rover watershed: the brand's first 'crossover SUV'. Sharing hardware with the Jaguar F-Pace in the wide JLR family, and the company's range of four- and six-cylinder power units (plus a supercharged 5-litre V8 for the near-insane SVR high-performance model). A subtly new, sculptural exterior 'design language' was devised by Gerry McGovern and his team to fuse sportiness with rugged fitness-for-purpose.

◄ Inside a 2018 Range Rover, where the chauffeured rear-sear passengers sat in opulence akin to a private jet.

◄ Petrol-electric drivetrain of the 2018 Range Rover plug-in hybrid.

➤ Range Rover L405s took to the historic Silk Road for a world-striding test run to coincide with the 2012 launch.

◄ Where it counted, in its ability to traverse the most testing of terrain, the fourth-generation Range Rover was masterful as ever.

⌃ Hybrid power helped lower the Range Rover's environmental impact, one area where the full-on fossil fuel cars of the past had never been strong ...

⌃ The second-generation of the hugely popular Range Rover Sport undergoing crucial stability testing.

➤➤ The Range Rover Sport Dynamic could hold its own in any driving conditions, snow included.

▲ A high-performance SVR version of the Range Rover Sport making its customary splash.

◄ Clockwise from left: the Velar's interior was rather more intimate than many traditional Range Rover owners had come to expect but certainly very airy; early design rendering for the Velar would point to a dramatic new direction for Range Rover; tighter, smoother, less bulky: the Velar was related to the correspondingly 'different' Jaguar F-Pace.

➤ The Velar name went back to the very genesis of Range Rover, and the new car helped ensure it stayed relevant in the twenty-first century.

Then, for 2019, the top-selling Range Rover Evoque received a complete technical rethink. Despite its flush-fitting door handles and slender LED headlights, the low-roof coupé profile so beloved by more than 750,000 Evoque buyers so far largely remained. The Premium Transverse Architecture structure, though, was totally new, built to cradle a variety of drivetrains which, as well as four-cylinder petrol and diesel engines, would include a 48-volt 'mild-hybrid' option that harvested deceleration energy to run the car in pure electric mode up to 11mph, and slash fuel consumption overall. A year away from the brand-new Evoque's launch would come a new plug-in electric hybrid model with a three-cylinder Ingenium petrol engine/electric motor combination.

Elsewhere, interesting new tech abounded, from cosseting seat fabrics woven with recycled plastics, to a rear-view mirror that turned into a rear video monitor camera if the driver's sight-line is blocked, and a 'Ground View' facility for the touch-screen scanning under the car to highlight rocks, or kerbs. The car cost £1 billion to develop.

How the tight-knit, industrious team who founded the Range Rover dynasty would react to the evolving nuances between all the different Range Rover models in the range as this is written will never be known. But the fact that Range Rovers are nearly unparalleled both on and off the road for power, prestige, presence and practicality remains testimony to their belief in creating the ultimate in dual-purpose motor cars – and a cornerstone for the car industry in Britain after 1.7 million Range Rovers have found adventurous buyers.

➤ A brand-new inner structure underpinned the 2019 Evoque, although the familiar profile was carefully retained.

▲ The new Evoque could be had with leather upholstery, or else with fabrics that were woven with recycled plastics.